THE CAGED BEAR SPIES THE ANGEL

other books by the author

POETRY
Dawn Visions
Burnt Heart/Ode to the War Dead
This Body of Black Light Gone Through the Diamond
The Desert is the Only Way Out
The Chronicles of Akhira
The Blind Beekeeper
Mars & Beyond
Laughing Buddha Weeping Sufi
Salt Prayers
Ramadan Sonnets
Psalms for the Brokenhearted
I Imagine a Lion
Coattails of the Saint
Abdallah Jones and the Disappearing-Dust Caper
Love is a Letter Burning in a High Wind
The Flame of Transformation Turns to Light
Underwater Galaxies
The Music Space
Cooked Oranges
Through Rose Colored Glasses
Like When You Wave at a Train and the Train Hoots Back at You
In the Realm of Neither
The Fire Eater's Lunchbreak
Millennial Prognostications
You Open a Door and it's a Starry Night
Where Death Goes
Shaking the Quicksilver Pool
The Perfect Orchestra
Sparrow on the Prophet's Tomb
A Maddening Disregard for the Passage of Time
Stretched Out on Amethysts
Invention of the Wheel
Sparks Off the Main Strike
Chants for the Beauty Feast
In Constant Incandescence
Holiday from the Perfect Crime
The Caged Bear Spies the Angel

THEATER / THE FLOATING LOTUS MAGIC OPERA COMPANY
The Walls Are Running Blood
Bliss Apocalypse

PROSE
Zen Rock Gardening
The Little Book of Zen
Zen Wisdom

THE CAGED BEAR
SPIES THE ANGEL

POEMS

August 30, 2010 – March 6, 2011

Daniel Abdal-Hayy Moore

The Ecstatic Exchange
2011
Philadelphia

The Caged Bear Spies the Angel
Copyright © 2011 Daniel Abdal-Hayy Moore
All rights reserved.
Printed in the United States of America

For quotes any longer than those for critical articles and reviews, contact:
The Ecstatic Exchange,
6470 Morris Park Road, Philadelphia, PA 19151-2403
email: abdalhayy@danielmoorepoetry.com

First Edition
ISBN:978-0-578-08512-8 (paper)
Published by *The Ecstatic Exchange*,
6470 Morris Park Road, Philadelphia, PA 19151-2403

Also available from The Ecstatic Exchange:
Knocking from Inside, poems by Tiel Aisha Ansari

Acknowledgments: *When the Portal Opened* was first published in Poetry Ink 2011 from Moonstone Arts Press, *Bullet* won the Nazim Hikmet Prize for 2011, and was first published in its chapbook.

Front and back cover art by Salihah Moore Kirby
Back cover photograph by Malika Moore

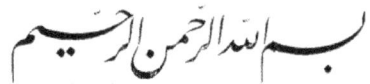

DEDICATION

To
Shaykh ibn al-Habib
(and the continuation of the Habibiyya)
Shaykh Bawa Muhaiyuddeen,
all shuyukh of instruction and ma'arifa,

to

Baji Tayyaba Khanum
of the unsounded depths

AND A SPECIAL DEDICATION TO
Douglas and Salihah Kirby
whose Path is
brilliantly unfolding

―――――

*The earth is not bereft
of Light*

CONTENTS

Author's Foreword   6
Don Quixote   11
The Color of The Lord   14
Seeking Sweetness   15
Sometimes Going to Sleep is Strange   17
Houses Turn into House-Shaped Dust   19
The Dark More Golden   21
Black Top White Top   24
The Luster of a Glisten   26
The Only Sound She Hears   28
Table   30
Duck's Back   33
When the Portal Opened   35
Bony Horse   37
Night Begins Early   39
How if We Haven't Left   42
If We Had a Choice   44
Inscriptions Among Ruins   47
The Light and the Dark of It   49
So Little Effort   50
I Heard the Angels   53
Black and Silver Angel   56
Hitting Bulls Eye   58
Lord of Introspection   60
The Bear Narrative   64
Grit   78
Ladder Leaned up Against the House   80
Single Contemplation   82
I'm Sailing Inward   84
The Shattering   86
Doors   89
I Haven't Said Anything Yet   91
Snow Deer   93
Multiplications and Subtractions   95

The Bear Narrative 2   97
Facing Inward   99
We Should All Be Very Happy   101
Cat Pounce   105
Obtrusion   110
Wet Black Nose   112
For Better or For Worse   114
Siren at Night   116
Love Flew by the Window   118
Clear Perspective   121
Today's the Day   124
Bread   127
Moments   130
Mother Time   134
Dancing on the Head of a Pin   137
The Most Tangible Songs of Our Hearts   140
The Radical Formation of Things   144
Spaghetti Noodles   147
The King Became His Breakfast   151
Radiance of Horses   153
It's Too Late to Save The Patient   155
There is No Distance   158
His Tight Embrace   163
Some Deaths   164
Tale of the Ten Doctors and a Snowman   166
Saint John of the Cross in Prison   170
Destiny Inside-Out   172
The Blind Night Watchman   179
Offshoots   182
The Knocking   186
Pastoral   190
Last Wish   193
A Stoppered Bottle   196

Index   198

AUTHOR'S FOREWORD

In one aspect this book of poems is a failure. I began with a title that I sensed would inspire a narrative of magic and transformation. Reality caught up with me, however, in that nearly at the end of the book I became the one transformed, either more or less into the caged bear. Time and a possible emergence from that cage will tell.

The tale starts out well enough, although I always conceived it more as a patchwork, rather than a sensible story from first thread throughout to a neat end. It would always be a kind of forest trail littered with brush and twigs of other obtruding lyrical outbursts, shards of this and that, and then the story might emerge again, in which a Prince, a Russian Prince at that, is actually transformed into the bear he first encounters on a hunt, and becomes something like the bear my daughter Salihah painted which adorns the cover of this book.

There is a chunk of a story of sorts in *The Bear Narrative*, and a second part a bit further along, but somehow the inspiration this time didn't catch fire as I thought it would, and the bear in the story finally traipses off on its own into the obscurity of this forest or that. And I'm left with path debris that forks here and there as well, in my usual fashion, hopefully not without lit focus and sparkly glimmers, but having nothing much whatever to do with bears or magical inter-species transformations.

Then along the way I found myself in the Emergency Room of a local hospital with a bleeding ulcer, and after the doctors entered into its rather gory domain, with a snip here and there, I was diagnosed with a gastric lymphoma, a mild one, with the old-fashioned soda fountain name of a MALT, without, I assume, the bent straws and blaring jukebox, easily combated with antibiotics and some radiation, I was told, in these days of higher cancer survival, may Allah be praised. Meanwhile, my daughter Salihah, newly in love with a musician named Douglas, was moving away pretty definitively from her home base in Philadelphia to live with him in Bolinas (where I in fact also lived in my early twenties for a year), above San Francisco on the Pacific Coast. He was coming to help her move, and we would meet him for the first time, and he would play music for a poetry reading and book launch I had arranged for, hiring a hall and sending out a number of printed invitations. I was admitted to the hospital the day before the event was to take place, and in the ICU with the tubes and beeps abounding aplenty until my diagnosis could be finalized, we had to cancel the event entirely. At this point, and not until much later, we didn't tell our daughter (one of the tenderest-hearted creatures I've ever known) of my diagnosis, for fear she would decide not to carry through in her move. But when they came to my room the night before leaving, Douglas said he wanted a deeper blessing, and I was putting my hands together to make a prayer, when he added, "We want you to marry us."

So following the way of Islam, where marriage is serious but not at all necessarily elaborate, with wife Malika and a surprised nurse as witnesses, I married them with proper vows, acceptable dowry and Qur'anic recitation, a hospital-bed wedding, of the most exalted kind... the room palpably elbow to elbow — and sparkling bright ones at that — with angels.

One of the latter poems, *It's Too Late to Save the Patient*, portends the illness to come, and the poems following until I was released were written during my stay in a bed you can't quite get a proper sleep in, whose blessed discomfort urges you to heal quickly and leave, out one exit or another. Till now, God has sent me out the life exit, to my continued amazement and my continual and profound gratitude.

For a man would not hesitate to spend all he had
if he only understood the secret of his own heart

If a man could but grasp the bliss of his secret
he would shed a tear with every breath he breathed.

Then, his body become his cage, he would fly from it
with the wings of contemplation to the Furthest Lote-Tree.

He would freely roam around the Throne and the Footstool
which make the heavenly bodies appear like a small ring.

He would see the planets and the secrets of their constellations
and the meaning of their tremendously rapid movement.

The veil of the Tablet of Forms would be lifted from his secret
and so the hidden knowledges would emerge uncovered.

Had the trees been the pens to write it and their ink
the surrounding seas, they would have dried up.
   — *from* The Greater Qasida, Shaykh Muhammad ibn al Habib

"The believer *(mu'min)* is such that when he closes his eyes in his head, the eyes of his heart are opened and he sees what is over there; and when he closes the eyes of his heart, the eyes in his head are opened and he sees the situation of Allah and His dealings with His creatures."
   — Shaykh 'Abd al-Qadir al-Jilani *(Utterances)*

DON QUIXOTE

In Orson Welles' version
Don Quixote strides up to the silver screen where

the film of a woman being attacked is being
projected and extending his sword to defend her

cuts it to shreds

No angel falls from a rooftop
who doesn't swoop away

The smudged city below looking sootier

Never underestimate the power of the
moment to change the universe

and not just explosions in distant-most
space

but beads on tabletops and
perspiration on foreheads

to suddenly be jewels

You hardly notice the passing of time
until it's too late

and then it starts all over again

I don't know why sleek horses always
ride right through the

middle of these poems

or why when I shoot strong water-spray
through the back garden gate to the

alley flowers I always
think of Rilke

There's no telling what we do
when left to our own devices

The knell of the closing day
the dark of the opening one

Then suddenly we're moving outlines
slowly taking shape

assuming what we see
is more than a projection

though when sliced to ribbons it
turns out to be true

The coat of many colors worn by Joseph
and hounded by wolves

until we see for ourselves
it's always God's Face

looking right at us

miracles under our thumbs
and inside our eyelids

No grander glade than
silvery grasses

No more gorgeous gulches
than throats of song

8/30

THE COLOR OF THE LORD

I picked out quarters
that could be kept bare

The horse in its stall
its whinny in the air

Where is the water
that will wash us

in the color of
the Lord?

8/30

SEEKING SWEETNESS

Rusted railway cars and a
basket of plucked ducks

don't diminish the necessary sunset
and become quite sacred in the

dark

We hold out our hands and
shouldn't be surprised at whatever

comes to them of God's bounty

If you're off to see the Wizard
don't forget to take your hat

lest he fancy your head on a plate
since wizards can be a

volatile lot

Note the passing landscape as you
go and the three and twenty

blackbirds spelling divine
sentences in their flight

I've seen a white sun spread its
beneficent rays

and a black moon frighten the
lesser owls

No ribbon of river runs backwards though
and Wile E. Coyote sniffs the trail as he

goes loping along
seeking sweetness

9/1

SOMETIMES GOING TO SLEEP IS STRANGE

Sometimes going to sleep is strange
like a boat rolling across dry land

as if departing from our perceptions into
an ambiguous dark cave

were not the sleep of infants
just out of the womb

but rather like a solid expected to melt
but staying on the surface as

implacable as ice

I put my head on the pillow
and felt heavily estranged from sleep

as if I wouldn't get down in there
into its tropical trough its

thatch of fuzziness that often suddenly
opens onto strangely fractured sunlight

where non-chronological vivid scenes take place
with some of their last dramatic remnants

surfacing at the point of waking or
unraveling entirely into a few stray

tastes and inklings

as if the great dream
elevator expelled us then sank

back down into the bed underground
connecting with previous episodes perhaps

and carrying on perfectly naturally
scene linked to scene but in

a now unreachable oblivion

9/7

HOUSES TURN INTO HOUSE-SHAPED DUST

Houses turn into house-shaped dust
and dust into trampling horses heading

south against gray wind

A strong breath blows across everything
at once though

nothing's obliterated but obliteration itself

The winking face at the window
continues unto eternity

Wheels squeaking on a road become
duck migrations to warmer climes

high above the heads of the hungry

Such a simple word to say
and so few able to say it

that inwardly we're all jungle folk
passing ripe and luscious fruits to

each other among the
lower branches as at home here

as if we'd descended from apes

But the soulful bright stars we were at the
beginning are the soulful bright stars we are

now
even in the worst light

It only takes a little nudge to enter
God's blissful precincts

It only takes a few bloody knees
and a broken heart

9/9

THE DARK MORE GOLDEN

*"It's cost me a lot
all this rowing and baling"*

said the one-eyed boatswain

The sun shone hot on the
Galapagos Islands and

sun-baked lizards shot long sticky
tongues at dragonflies in

hot breezes

Of course none of this exists

Or we could try
The ancient Chinese poet stood and

*stuffed his newest poem in his
sleeve and laughed at the waterfall*

Yet he wasn't ancient while alive
though he died at sixty-five

He's only ancient these many long
centuries later

He's real
You can read his poems in a book

Also real may be
the whinny of a flying horse

and its glorious liftoff from earth
with the Prophet (peace be upon him)

astride it

Now there's a picture worth gazing at
as the night stars make concentric

circles round his blessed head as he
goes from Mecca to Jerusalem

noting everything passing and to come
in his celestial gallop through

night mists and night clarities

We sit at tables in chairs and
walk upright in streets between trees

pulling on and off our clothing

exchanging glances and a few choice words
just as everyone has ever done

with the same uncanny sensation afterwards
or even during

(for the hopelessly in love with God and the

hopefully enlightened)

that we may not exist at all in
any true substantial sense

but the Light of us does
and strikes deliriously gorgeous

pictures off us like
sparks off a forge

making light less dark
and the dark more golden

9/11

BLACK TOP WHITE TOP

A black top with a star ablaze on
top of it spins at the top

of the world

A white top with moon aglow on the
bottom of it spins at the

bottom of the world

They're kept spinning in
place by two giant angels put there

for that purpose
who brood over the world and fold and

unfold their gigantic wings while

keeping the two tops going
round and round for the

equilibrium of the axis

Their faces are almost
discernible in the clouds

They have names but
languages can't pronounce them

They call out to each other from
time to time round the

global bulge

But they're most content
giving their top a spin from

time to time
and by it

keeping the earth
going round

and round

9/12

THE LUSTER OF A GLISTEN

The luster of a glisten is
enough to elicit bliss

The gleam from a beam
enough to confound the intellect

The crack of a rock in a creek
can take us back to where

we lost track

The whiff of a sniff can lift
even the most morose heart

from the hotbed of heartbreak

All these phenomena
splinter and splatter in

this world to focus from the
unseen world onto this one

some hint of the high rainbowing
laughter to come

some sparkle that pointillists
darkness into dots both

clustered and spaced out enough to

glimpse His Face as it bends toward us

with cool eyes ablaze always
seeing into our cranny suddenly

overpoured with Light

9/13

THE ONLY SOUND SHE HEARS

When everything's quiet
can you hear the loon from

across the lake

the soft snore of a woodchuck snoozing

the death of a firefly?

A house creak settling into
its foundations?

A window making itself even
more transparent for the beloved to

see down the road for her lover
clipcloppiting up on horseback

though no horse exists for
miles around

and he's been gone for over a year now?

Earth turns with its trillion wheels
making a little squeak against its clouds

Clouds themselves sizzle in
space a little as they disintegrate

or hum huge chords as they accumulate over
oceans that endlessly

slosh below them
holding in their aqueous bodies

unearthly symphonies of clicks and
deep groans beneath their

watery surfaces

through which her love will never
rise again though her eyes themselves

become windows finally filming over

and he jump down from his horse
(she can hear his feet hit gravel)

and the sound of earth turning in its
ocean of stars become

the only sound she hears

TABLE

1

A delectable table is set for any
guests out of unknown or

imaginal worlds to emerge and
partake of equally effervescent and

evanescent realities

but while here assemble on
chairs and bless the meal they're

about to take in their most
transparent partaking

Don Quixote appears out of his
ambiguous transitional world of

Spain between Muslim and Christian
in the ripped open air of

expulsions and inquisitions

seeing past glory as he
surveys the seated guests from

Socrates onward in their

glorious technicolor exploits and
least triumphs trumpeted in his

imagination to great heights

2

It's madder to think we're all not
on the Great Journey toward

that which is right here with us now
seen through to its Source and its

Glorious Lord from the
meanest crumb to the

grandest gesture against a
backdrop of high mountains and

encircling stars

3

This is the table the whole world
sits at and all time includes

at which we are both
host and guest

entertaining no notions
at the true heart of us but

true notions

enticing richest aromas from
everything before us

seeing before us not the cruel world
but God's world

in spite of its cruelty

passing to our right and left
nutritious substances and their

gravies and the gilded strawberries of
immediate delight

dipped in the rare chocolates of

sobriety's darker hues

9/20

DUCK'S BACK

I thank the Lord for my
bed like a boat that

rocks me to sleep

from which I've jut gotten up to
write this down

And thank the Lord for both
up and down either literally or

figuratively when ascending a
scale or spiritual ladder or

diving either deeper into ourselves or
deep into sleep as I just did for a

short afternoon nap with
sore feet and a bandaged ear

for which I also thank the Lord
both for feet however sharp the

heel pain and ear however that pesky
basal cell carcinoma recently excised

got in there

And thank the Lord for our ability to

thank through all duress in any of its

cleansing downpours
wet with it and drenched with it however

it and He may wish to drench us
through and through as only

duck's back water under from which we may
waggle our tail feathers and

waddle or flap away

9/21

WHEN THE PORTAL OPENED

When the portal opened and we
saw the queen taking her tea the

usual way with cup in hand and
lips pursed

we knew we now knew something few knew

and went from there disencumbered by
that much at least in knowing

Then the white horse appeared with no
rider and nudged a door open and

came into the house all ashimmer
an angel astride it

And we suddenly knew we now knew
something few knew and we

couldn't perfectly tell them though
we'd try to extend our knowing

At last it was time to leave this earth
having seen and heard all we were

allotted to see and hear of knowing
and the great dark tent was

lifted away showing us things in all their
glorious colors and all their original shapes

and we then knew we knew what even
we couldn't know of knowing

and that it was time to go to
know what none could know

but Him the Knower of all there
is to know

of knowing

9/21

BONY HORSE

We all ride a bony horse
into illusory adventures

hallowing the empty air
with our empty phrases

delivered in high rhetorical mode
to any who'll listen

Tilting at windmills
is only the half of it

When we lie bruised and
broken in our battered armor

what comfort do we get
from the nearest comforter

but mist surrounds us
the compassionate mist

out from which might ride
further adversaries or further helpers

none though as close as our own
jugular vein

as windmill blades turn like
infernal sails above us

wind making flapping sounds
and the donkey braying

our horse's closest companion
at this point in our story

9/23

NIGHT BEGINS EARLY

Night begins early for the saint
united in intimate friendship

It begins with rose hips on their stems
acres of rose gardens folded

inside their glossy spheres

It begins with the saint
opening just-born eyes

letting daylight
loose into the world

It begins with continents
as one continuous land

seas as one continuous water

when stars didn't disappear in sunlight
but shone by day

in the saint's eyes

The saint's intimate friendship with the
Friend by Whom each saint is

friend of the Friend and by eternity's
light befriended

Each unfolding on earth
his actual eyelids opening

Each thump or throb in forest or town
at crossroad or crosswalk

his actual heartbeats thumping

Each silent movement of his silvery lips
actual water sliding under bridges

And when his whispers are answered
massive flamingo flights over the Sahara

in a *whoosh* of pink radiance

And when God remains unanswering
Amazonian toucans in tangled trees

turn silently watchful

We see him in our minds' eyes
sitting from a short nap

surrounded by alive atmospheres
exhaled and inhaled

by the Friend by Whose close Friendship
each friend is

so closely

befriended

once each moment in each new eternity born
from the Friend's close detachment

and the saint's intimacy
born each moment

in the Friend's close detachment

9/24

HOW IF WE HAVEN'T LEFT

How if we haven't left the home of our bones
can we hope to return to the

home of our heart?

Skeletons with an inside glow
watch us go from the side of the road

Behind them stretch the unknown forests
that surround us on every side

forests of the Unknown with leaves in
shapes of leopards and trees in the

shapes of light

How can we go knowing all this
when the slightest breeze ripples the

lake with messages of water?

All that can be heard is the
drip of the first drop that

fell straight down into a bigger drop

Camels in a long string of distant silhouettes
heading in all one direction

slowly achieving it by their
up and down motion

Visualize the complete poem that speaks
directly to God without the

paraphernalia of mortality or immortality
yet is in this hesitant speech after all

that we place on the taut string to
shoot to His precincts imagined distant

but which are instantly intimate

and to hit the target of our
own hearts to achieve the central

eye into which the arrow-point enters
atom by atom and molecule by molecule

to cure us of all ill

9/28

IF WE HAD A CHOICE

If we had a choice of how to
leave this world how would we

choose *(ruling out suicide)* would it be

a door our exact body shape coming
around us so gently as if

stepping into a warm bath and we would
slip up through the body shape as if we were

waking from a nap into a room flooded with
sunlight?

Or in a boat down a cobalt blue river into an
ocean as much air as water or color as

darkness and a certain intelligent dissolution might

take place like powder into a mixture
or an exhalation into a breeze already

going that way?

Let's rule out any kind of violence say of the
locomotive crushing-us-tied-to-the-tracks kind

or agony in a hospital bed octupusedly
linked up by myriad transparent tubes to

myriad machines

Out walking for example by a beloved vista
in the woods among grazing deer who

look up with soft loving eyes as we
simply disappear between trees

Not by falling overboard by losing our
earthly balance from this

world to the next though it may in fact be
more like that than say running through a

sprinklers naked and not coming out again
ever

It's transference from one dimension to
another neither one less

blessed than the other but the
act of transitioning is fraught with certain

sensational anxieties as if
getting coiled in death-dragon's

iron plated skin spiraled in fire is
assumed to be the normal

vehicle of next-world teleportation from ancient
times to now —

...or by gazing say into a mirror
in a totally non-Narcissistic way

we suddenly are
no longer on this side at all

and on that side
we just walk away?

                                        9/30

INSCRIPTIONS AMONG RUINS

The inscription on the wall says
"As we age
walls are less substantial

We crumble at the same rate"

On a tiny Egyptian glass bottle half-
buried in sand an inscription reads
"When you discover me
I'll be gone"

On floor tiles written in mosaics
an inscription reads
"Walk across me
Where will it get you?"

Another further along says
"You're here now
Don't look back"

Another turning off to the right says
"If this is a decision
walk wisely"

Entering ruins of the main hall
on a ceiling beam fallen among
rubble it says
"When high enjoy the view
When low that you're still alive"

On a windowsill looking out onto
Gem Smoking Mountain the inscription reads
"One glance is enough
to confirm
the Unseen"

At the end of a corridor exit
covered over or that
never opened out it says
"Having reached this far
Why are you here?"

On a trail leading away from the ruins
on a stone scattered
haphazardly among stones it says
"Say goodbye
to what you never knew"

                                                                10/2

THE LIGHT AND THE DARK OF IT

Dream images litter our shore
where those multicolored boats are

Van Gogh painted

In miniature the world comes into
being and goes out again

under a microscope looking for proof

When windows are swung open
the garden comes into the room

Maybe even Adam and Eve

How is our consciousness a repository
for every kind of thing

the light and the dark of it
going on forever?

10/6

SO LITTLE EFFORT

There once was a man who tipped his hat
and out fell bird's eggs

How they got there was nobody's guess
but God's to know

Once a man stepped out of them and trees
grew from his shoes

The shoes are gone but the roots are
long and the tree shades his house

*How can we attribute anything to anything at all
and not to God?*

No conception contains Him but really
every squeal and tweedle audible or

inaudible is something rare and
strange with kaleidoscopic colorations and

a falling together of the most splendid elements
from racing gray hounds to a sudden

standstill in the middle of a field of an
entire herd of sheep

until they go back to their munching

A woman got up one morning and
never stopped climbing

They say she's at the ninety-ninth level about now
watering the universe with her

tears her good will and a little silver
watering can that never runs dry

I sometimes wonder what we're waiting for
then go back to whatever it was I was

doing

On the one hand waiting
on the other a great rush toward and

through us of everything we're decreed to see

It's not so mysterious nor even in one sense
theological

It simply is

The forest opens up like the halves of a melon
and all its billion leaves are shining

Our little trails on the ground one time
covered with tiny golden leaf-shaped

diary pages of the tree's hot season

now scattered at their roots like
school girls having left their homework to

run off to play

There once was a man and a woman
who saw each other through a

latticework of purity and when their
marriage was ordained a drop from

heaven landed on the canvas slope of a white tent
and ran down it to water what grew to

remind us all of the incessant
incandescent bounty we

obtain with so little effort

10/7

I HEARD THE ANGELS

I heard the angels'

high-pitched singing

Puts all western music to shame with

all its sawing and soaring

A twirl of unworldly voices
or as if fish in the sea opened their

throats just below the surface
and communicated with a distant

galaxy and the galaxy communicated back

O sweet machinery!

Grass turning up as it's bent by a
trillion breezes then

blown by a wind

each blade an aerated conch shell blast
so etherially announcing a

stately procession of no known but
highly knowing creature on its

rounds of subatomic inspection each
material atom at its absolute

shiniest and each immaterial atom
at its brilliant peak of

immateriality so high-tension in its
solitude it has to sing!

Grind of the
immaterial against itself

causing such delicious squeaking!

Subatomic choirs released
from their silence

the hallelujahs of edges
where one thing seems to stop and

another start

Staggering sunlight above the
Sahara

The syncopation of each sand-grain
the granulated bass notes of them

lying so lightly on the land
then lifted twirlescently by a wind

and landing in threnody recapitulation
melody by melody

as if clouds conducted them
in a near-white sky

As if we opened our mouths
and out came inaudible song

                                                    10/8

BLACK AND SILVER ANGEL

Love is a black and silver
angel with fiery acorn for a head

who comes into us with sparklers from
below and spirals up lighting up

floors and stairways to mysterious
landings and moonlit balconies we never before knew

existed in us with the lacy curtains of our
childhoods pulled back revealing the

black and silver drapes of love's more
winding and labyrinthine corridors

beckoning to us by their futurity down
one road or another to taste both

the journey and its anticipated arrival

as the black and silver angel goes
with a detached air away to

smite another soul with love's arising
corkscrew

and lulls another into self-love only

but turns our eyes like beacons across

treacherous rocks to sunrise horizons

where flaming sails are seen in silhouette
before a gradually lightening

bright blue sky before
night comes again and blackens us with its

deep angelic silver

                                                             10/16

HITTING BULLS EYE

In memoriam Shaykh Mansur Escudero

Marked from the start as one who would
fly from a taut bowstring and

hit bulls eye
cutting through every air

Who would distribute sweet heartbeats with
every encounter

on Pasha mountain peak or dustbowl
OK Corral

Closing gaps wherever they appear
and opening them in some places

God-blessed from the start but making no
show of it

in horse-dust rising around us all or
star-silver sprinkling through the trees we

stand among

Both passenger and boatman
oarsman and overseer

Marked from the start by indescribable processes

to stand or sit among us in

pure blessedness
as if leaning from a sublimer dimension

into our own

Whose death is more an appearance among us
free of all uncertainty

leaving in us a sense of our own
blessedness

expanding that dimension
into our own

with an amber glow of interstellar light

Showing the path trod
and the goal engraved

Arrow of the straight shot
and the clean arrival

Marked from the start as one who would
sing at the taut bow's release

across intervening air
and hit bulls eye

God's open Eyes
closed around him now

10/16

LORD OF INTROSPECTION

May the Lord of Introspection meet us at the
inner gate and take us deeper in to where

existence is essentialized to its
sleekest denominators whose interactions

make a charming rustic music
and many slow-moving beasts with human faces

pass inquisitively by casting us
poignant glances with their huge

watery eyes

Deeper deeper in than we've ever gone before
across electrified gorges crossing

rope bridges pulled taut above cascading waterfalls
of fire and ice

or in other words past every menacing or
formidable material manifestation as their

well-guarded chambers give way magnificently to
rideable elements whose manes are

streaming silver

(How hard it is to get to this without

evoking phantasmal entities or inert
abstractions)

The Lord of Introspection with perfect equanimity
whose perfect equanimity is what

leads us with its air of musk and liquid amber
to enter into serious recognitions of

stillness

This is where now everything is a flat and
placid ocean so quicksilver in its

purest horizontality it reflects the entire
heavens in one tidal blink

and every speck that falls through air
is divinely defined as it falls

arriving at its soft landing on the
still ocean's surface under beams that

simply undulate above it

I call in at this point to hear
an answer back

The whole universe turned inside-out now
without disturbing a single atom

where every terrible thing is a
sparkling stream over whose reflective surface pass

slowly suspended exotic birds whose
feathers' motions generate the

pictures we see in momentary visualizations
taken lock stock and barrel as

reality

The picture changes and never changes
as tumult leads to sublimity and

back again to its raw footage where
people seem to perish and whose

civilizations shout their final worth
as greater waves engulf them

a silver funnel drawing us all down

I cry out to the angels on the battlements
who pass chunks of light through

sulfurous clouds themselves calling out
each to each in incomprehensible sweet

languages everything in creation seems to
understand but us

O Lord of Introspection take us
further in and further down

than normal breath allows

                                                        10/17

THE BEAR NARRATIVE

1

A bear wandered in the forest who was
both a bear and not a bear

in that he was a bewitched Prince
probably with a grand aristocratic

name like Vaslav Archovaski
whose family back in Saint Petersburg have

given him up for lost after the
deer hunt gone bad over a

year ago as they sit in their elegant
dacha filled with heavy furniture

and drink all day out of deep purple glasses
lamenting the end of their dynasty

while Vaslav never getting used to such
big paws and curved claws

stands in a cascade grabbing
fish out of the water he sees in the

shrill glisten out of those
two beady eyes of his

2

The reason for the bewitching is not clear
certainly not to Vaslav

He wracks his poor bear brains every day
going over all the details of his

former hairless existence
to know where he could have

earned or deserved his present
shaggy and shambling condition

although he's always been fond of slightly
underdone trout

3

The sweet sweet sound of the
clarion horn over the

misty valley and the bear hunt is on

The counts and brigadiers on their
fine horses move out in a line

The mist ahead almost cookie-cutter
shapes barely bear-like in various

directions but no one raises their
guns in a quiet so intense you might hear

bear's breath ahead huffing its exhalations

Vaslav Archovaski in his new
hunting jacket with moose-bone buttons

sent all the way from Ontario
sits tall in his saddle with fresh memories of

Matilde *(French pronunciation)* on his lips
as the morning chill works its

way inside his jacket against his
woolen inner shirt

*"Vaslav you wonderful hunter of hearts you
sweet pumpkin I know you'll*

excel tomorrow at the hunt

*No bear in his right mind would
cross your path!"*

4

But a bear in its right mind did
cross his path the very elegant

dew-diamonded path of Vaslav Archovaski
that fateful morning

and that right-minded bear stood up in
circus fashion on its hind legs and sat

immediately down again with hind legs straight
out in front of it and looked with its

bear eyes eye to eye with our Prince
who stopped his horse in his tracks to see

such a personable display of civility on
such a wild creature's natural heart

It seemed the bear all five or six hundred
shaggy pounds of him or her was most

interested in an early morning conversation
than to menace our Prince with

eons of raw bear brutishness and sharp
teeth or to be shot at once and made into

bear meat and bear trophy on the
fireplace wall in the billiard room of the

palace

5

What is it to see the world
out a bear's eyes?

What does he see?

Glisten and ripple of sunlight on shade

Darkness dimensionally folding into itself ever
invitingly deeper?

Splash and flash that might yield a fish?

Night coming on with squint into blackness
too far away to see stars?

One thing then another
over there where the

sound came from?

Something curious and gorgeous
makes my stomach rumble

Plod over there and have a look

Look down the cliff side to
green valleys for a second

Continue onward

to somewhere

Have a seat

Go to sleep

6

But this bear looked Prince Vaslav
Petrovich Ivanovich Stanislav Archovaski

directly in the eyes
training its eyes which glistened like two

moist cranberries in the misty light

and said in clear and elegant speech
"Your conceptions have always

fallen short" and then just looked at him
its front paws suspended in

front of its chest as if to hold out a
tray of sweetmeats

The Prince's horse snorted
and for a moment the Prince thought it

was snorting in agreement

The bear continued
"From intimate ideas about your

own self to conceptions of other people
to the world and how it's

put together and how it
works to the vaster unseen world

that holds this
world the way a concerned and

careful mother holds her newborn cub
close to her breast"

Branches in the forest fell and
cracked around them

The Prince could hear a distant
river gurgle

The bear flicked a fly away from its
face

Was it wearing a short jacket and
velvet pants?

No
just the light falling on its fur

"Even your appreciation of this moment is

not only faulty but almost totally

*non-existent since you've ruled out
animals making any kind of sense*

*and bears especially and my speaking to you in
this way totally confounds you"*

The horse lowered its head and
munched some grass as if to say

*It looks like
we'll be here for a while*

Finally the Prince cleared his throat and for the
first time noticed how dry it had

become

"Now see here bear" he began
rolling his "r's" just right

as if addressing a grandparent at court
though there was a hint of

challenge in his voice

*"Now you see here Prince Vaslav for
once in your life and see that*

here's a golden opportunity to open

*gates to floods of light you've
never even considered before"*

The bear stood up on its four legs and
very slowly took a few steps

toward the Prince and his horse
which kept on grazing

Ambled right up to the pair
as close as your stretched out hand

until the breath from its black nostrils
puffed in little steam clouds and

hung for a moment in the air
between them and the Prince could

actually smell the bear's lush breath in the
falling light

The Prince suddenly became aware of
just how huge the bear was and how

long were its black claws and how
lustrous in the light was its

dark sable coat and how
grand it would look on the

billiard room wall and how utterly

out of the question it was unless the

Prince was dreaming all this or had simply gone
momentarily crazy

Finally the bear said nonchalantly
picking up a twig in its claws and

inspecting it in front of what the
Prince thought seemed to be

nearsighted eyes

*"Let's take the long view my dear Prince Vaslav
if we can*

*and I'll give you some time to
put all this in some kind of*

perspective"

The bear shot the Prince a
glance as if checking to see if he was

following the thought stream or had gone
almost completely unconscious

But Vaslav was in fact in a state of the most
openly receptive shock in his life

He could feel his ears tingle and thought his

hair might be electrified and

sticking straight out from his head

Now the bear lay down beside the
horse and seemed to lean on one

elbow supporting its big head on
its paw

"No hurry" it said to the Prince
"we've got plenty of time"

7

Then the bear did something that Vaslav
forever after marveled at

The bear looked down at a cluster of
berries growing by its elbow

It huffed a kind of affable growl and
reached down and picked a

bunch of them

They almost glowed a kind of
lurid orange with crimson touches

Bear looked once across at Vaslav on his horse

then extended the branch

*"Here great Prince
have a chew on these and let's*

see where it takes us"

The bear seeing the space between them
put the branch with the berries in its

teeth and got up on its haunches and
leaned way toward Vaslav who was

again amazed at the bear's size
for in one gesture

its huge head was right up to
Vaslav's hand still gripping his

now utterly peaceful horse's reins

"Chew them slowly" the bear said then
it let go of them and with a

sudden burst of bear's breath
turned and went back to its

reclining position
steadily eyeing the Prince through half

squinting bear eyes

Prince Vaslav had no choice but
the berries had an intoxicating odor and

glowed ever more redly now as he
held them

He took a bite of one and its
deliciousness overwhelmed him

For in a glance he was in his own
banquet room at a feast day

the tables laden with gigantic
displays of fruits of every conceivable

kind though in this quick vision
each display seemed to be arranged or

sculpted as figures of bears in various
bear-like positions

Vaslav let his teeth sink in and bit down

Floods of golden juice filled his
mouth

He ate another
and heard the bear sniff steamily in approval

He ate them all
and the stillness of the forest became

the hunched fold of a stillness only
a crack of branch or rustle of

leaves interrupts
and then a stillness like

water in a disturbed pond
covering over the sound and

expanding ever wider through the
late sun-dappled trees in that

tableau of Prince on horse and
mountain of bear at his feet

almost dozing off as Prince Vaslav
Petrovich Ivanovich Stanislav Archovaski's

entire life flashes before him but in
musical phrases and illuminated

pictures in serenely rapid motion
as a seed case falls on a

log nearby and clangs curiously
through that remote forest on a

faraway hill surrounded by a
now more golden mist

in which our characters remain for now
ingesting their divine salivas

10/29- 11/13

GRIT

I have a sensation of floating
losing balance to

regain it elsewhere

On the tilted deck of the Titanic?

A sliding dance floor?
Some earthless place

beyond the grave?

Ah
to grow old we have the ancient

Chinese Poets

their glittering eyes drifting whiskers
rustling streams misty

mountaintops

Or those indefatigable Moroccan seventy- or
eighty-year old Sufis who'd traveled for

weeks from their
villages on their donkeys and slid

off them at the Master's Meknes zawiyya

to spend the next three days and
nights in vigorous dances for Allah

while we younger acolytes would have to
sit out a few to catch our breath

while these old coots
went on and on

These old coots seemed superhuman
or rather to be most truthful

these old coots were
held up in Allah's Endlessness

as that embrace of His
was all their longevity

and their
grit

11/14

LADDER LEANED UP AGAINST THE HOUSE

Though he couldn't see it from below
the man was astonished that the

ladder he'd leaned up against the house
extended into the clouds so he

climbed and climbed until he totally
disappeared

and from a certain point in the sky had the
sensation he was climbing down

gravity pulling him actually upward
in a cloud-ship's harbor so vast he

couldn't see them as hulls banked as they
were and piled on each other

to the top of space

He stepped down onto the ground and
marveled at its springiness its rainbowing arch

Birds wheeled upside down in a
yellow sky that flashed alternately

silver then gold

A distant calliope could also have been

his own breathing since a mile-high snow-deep

silence reigned everywhere

*After the initial image of this poem I was actually going to
pursue the idea that once we've*

*embarked on a Path and some progress is being
made a quantum*

*leap extension or even flight takes
place by Allah beyond our pale*

*capabilities for success
a roller coastering thrust that uplifts the*

*fragile but gaudy car of the selves we're in
to see ourselves now sailing across a*

*canyon whose fluctuating abalone colors are
actual angel song*

"Nearer my God to Thee"
our own disaster become

*an averted disaster
epiphany*

11/16

SINGLE CONTEMPLATION

The pool is crowded with
tiny sea urchins but when you

lean to look in you see it
also has the sky

Not as vast as the whole sky perhaps
but any portion of sky is in another way

the whole sky

Clouds puff across its pure blue
and craning a bit there is

the sun
its gaseous biliousness intact

and the sea urchins don't
seem to notice

though they might be
basking in the heat of the one

behind you

And when you look in again
you are in there too

Maybe not all of you

more the top of your body

and above you
the sky

God may lean in and
see us in much the same way

Except from every direction at once
and always the totality

from heart outward
and back again

No star of sky behind us
left out of the constellation

Day and night the same

every pool at once
in a single contemplation

11/20

I'M SAILING INWARD

I'm sailing inward
on a boat of breath

one skiff set sail against sunset

one sail catching sunset's scarlet

or going down in flames

standing still as light
against the mast

or sailing inward with a fleet of boats
some tugs some subs some rafts or

just a few boards lashed together

and one or two just twigs that
barely float

into the dark tunnel
into the slow maelstrom

I carry all the tatters and
ropes of my cargo

the miscommunications in a high wind
when our words are blown back at us

and the force of them lost in the
greater howling

But there's a magnificence in our
sailing inward no landlocked

soul can know

and the boat may smash on the
rocks at any moment

and splinters be all that's left
flecked with the paint of our craft

reminders of their phantom form

and the astrolabe that enabled us
to embrace the stars

11/24

THE SHATTERING

It's a shattering
but one that can take place in

slow motion or over a whole lifetime
or a most blessed or most cursed

instant in time
the constituents exploding or imploding

and only the eyes kept in focus the
undistracted pivot as all other

fragments fly in their
centrifugal or centripetal

spiral or else the heart itself
like a placid Himalaya

maintains its majestic ardor touching
between earth and sky those

ecstatically pewter clouds
magnifying light surrounding them

like mirrors in the Queen's boudoir
or the Sun King's extravagance

The shattering we fear and that
redeems us

tears us fiber by fiber as if
splitting bamboo

*(and may their pointed nibs become
calligrapher's pens)*

that leaves intact only the essential
spark from which all further

conflagration feeds

The insane hermit on the hill
sees in a sunrise the hinges of

cosmic wonder pull and bend
and sing in the sound of their

bending
and sees in the sunbeam as it

comes down atom by atom
the ladder that goes up

and takes aspiration continually
up with it

A shattering
where we might not recognize ourselves

coming back until
seated again on the rock from which we

began
in a still garden of

similar rocks
each shattered fragment in the rising

spiral containing
the whole

                                                        11/25

DOORS

If you hammer three times on the
door

and the first time hear only cacophonous
music and a sound of something

going down stairs in huge boots

And the second time windows
bang open in a whinnying wind

and furious leaves leave furious trees
from inside the house

And the third time a deathly silence answers
or three knocks knock back at you from

inside then maybe it's
the wrong door down the

wrong street in the wrong city in a
wrong world altogether without

horses on bright green hillsides in a
fine rain

or flakes of light accumulating like
snow in drifts where

no snow goes

How many doors in a silken silvery mountain
turn out to be rock?

How many turn out to be waterfalls across
the endless valve corridor into the heart?

There's a glimpse there of a sunlit place
of pure placid lakes and birds

falling on updrafts to spiral
away

Each piece of furniture in our hallowed place can be a
hindrance or a help

as we gaze forehead to forehead
at the stars in all their rotational expanse

Each piece of sky that lays across our
eyes a patchwork glimpse of

God's entirety in a human-sized frame

The only knockable doors
our inside doors that

turn inward and were
open all along

11/27

I HAVEN'T SAID ANYTHING YET

"I haven't said anything yet"
announced the ancient who'd been

talking all his life
so much so owls roosted in the black and

gnarly branches of his words

*"And I can just now get a
glimpse of what I might say"*

he squinted
and we saw high puffy clouds

scurrying away above his head

"one word at a time" he
continued

one word at a time
and some had rocks piled around their

base and some had moss already
growing on the sunny side

*"But my words may not be the
ones you're looking for in

all this debris"* he said as

brown leaves spiraled down onto

the bric-a-brac all around us
constantly changing and constantly

staying the same

"Yet if I did speak"
and in the distance heard a

peacock cry
"and my heart had expelled

all its ghosts" now his
facial features grew watery and his

voice from seemingly
far away

*"I might say how
happy and grateful I've been*

just to be here"
and at this point

disappeared
and we saw grass blades

eloquently shiver
where he'd just

been

12/3

SNOW DEER

The silver antlers of the snow deer
almost reflect back

planetary motions in their happy orbits

the all-white stag barely standing out
against the snow

His hooves might be diamond
but his great black eyes are

wary of each falling flake

He stands on a high cliff
looking out and down

The sky as well is almost
totally white and the

frozen river makes no sound save
occasional ice-crack

*(I'm warm writing this
but the air around me now is*

glassily chilled)

Someone approaches the deer
who now seems to have been waiting

for this very person showing no
impatience nor wild nervousness of

flight but stands stock
still in the whiteness

The man or woman
climbs on his back

There's a sound of flutes

The stag lurches off
from the cliff

into white sky

God's breath
nearby

12/3

MULTIPLICATIONS AND SUBTRACTIONS

Multiplications and subtractions go
merrily along adding

crows to a cornfield and bats across the
sky in an African twilight

goose bumps on the winner of the Miss America Pageant and
termites invading a neighboring termitary in a

distant rainforest in the Amazon

and as the numbers in all directions
pile up and bifurcate as well as

diminish and almost disappear above the
uncountable waves of choppy seas

singers to God on shorelines and in
deep interiors though numbering in the

millions raise their pure voices above the
cracks of tigers through bamboo groves and

laughing women and children washing clothes in
rushing Himalayan streams

to direct the throbbing marimbas of their
hearts to that same almost indefinable

essence whose single Light though more
diffuse than anything in nature

pervades everything at a single stroke and with
a single exclamation of wonder emits such

grateful babbling

                                                                    12/3

THE BEAR NARRATIVE 2

The bear drew a moustache across his
face across his already

hairy face

and drew on gloves as one might
draw on gloves before going to the

opera one finger at a time
and stood up and glanced at the

sky with a certain insouciance then
did a little shuffle a little

Thelonious Monk shuffle making a
strange sound in the forest of a

rhythmic crackle among the underbrush and
pine needles at his feet moving his

entire giant body lithely back and
forth like a really smaller mammal

and the sun made his
eyes twinkle and a few

gnats made his nose twitch
which he shook off with a

fly whisk like some African chief

(though where he got the whisk from is
anyone's guess)

Stylish light on his feet
eccentric and proud our bear waltzed

out of the
little forest glade leaving our

Prince gape-mouthed and confused the

first time in his life when suddenly
nothing quite made sense

always an enviable reflection and most valuable
interim toward wisdom

12/12

FACING INWARD

Every solitude sitting by itself
somewhere in the city

by a window or a door
or somewhere in the middle

of a room thatched by crossing ferns
by a soft river almost soundlessly passing

near a meadow where stags clang horns
when does are in heat

while raccoons go about their
business of banditry

and taxicabs screech to a halt
and start up again

until dawn

Then our solitudes expand and widen
over a larger shadowy territory

encompassing other solitudes
entering areas of other edges

other essences

until everywhere solitudes overlap

and the soundless river begins to

sound again over the rocks
in each other's areas endlessly

overlapping down through which the
annunciating angel calls us

each one by name
to enter originality

once and for all

facing inward

                                                            12/18

WE SHOULD ALL BE VERY HAPPY

> *Plunge in the ocean of obliteration— you might see Me*
> *Prepare to meet Me in the end with confidence*
> — Shaykh Shadhili

They searched between trees

Spaces where some sky shone

Sky containing sun by day and the
entire cosmos of stars by night

They searched between stars

Between sunrise and moonrise

They couldn't see God with the naked eye

Into centers of orchids

Into the workings of gnats' brains

Between each tick of the clock

But God was nowhere to be found

The focus of their eyes had become
so acute they thought they saw into

the very heart of matter

deep in each atom and even from the
first enormous exhalation of atoms

They scoured the place for traces

They double-checked their notes

Their notes said God was nowhere to be found

that when they died there was nothing

They narrowed their eyes to better see
the nothing to come

They tallied their notes and spread them
out before them

A river of wind came along and
took everything with it

Even the idea of God was
swept away in its rush

What confronted them now was a
giant door

One touch pushed it open

It opened onto a garden

The garden was made up of the most

delicate tendrils of nothingness

Tiny spiders disgorged frail webs

Excellent birds flew into the void

Everything looked turned inside-out

Nothing was left out of the inside nor inside the outside

It was all as fine as a hair

The hair fluttered in the wind

The wind passed through the hair and left it alone

There was neither silence nor noise

The head of something kept
faintly appearing

The voice in the air that was heard
was not a voice you could hear

A stern resilience to thought set in

Everything moved a giant step
forward in that space

A door opened that had no wall

Who is He Who has called us in?

A flea bites a man on the scalp
and raises a welt

A flea out of nowhere goes
back into nowhere

filled with our blood

I can't imagine this any more than I can
let it go

She came with a letter from the
original and read it out loud

If we didn't have to be born and die
God would have to

do it for us

To see God
throw down your eyes

Are you happy now?

We should all be
very happy

CAT POUNCE

Upon reality
the scarecrow hangs his arms

his drawn face saying nothing

We can scream and shout
and snow-capped mountains

stay the same

The freight train slows then
hastens to its goal

but not everyone aboard
knows for sure

Only the strapped-on tractors and tanks
are confident of their future

though the sound of the tracks clacking
doesn't affect them

put them to sleep nor
wake them

Sheep in the meadow
chew grass contentedly

Angels of life and death may

pass before their eyes'

rectangular pupils
but grass-chewing is their

primary occupation

A gleaming mahogany table
reflects back to themselves

faces of world leaders come together
to decide on such matters as man's

fate and mortality
but how many see themselves and

reflect on their transience
or how many of us do?

Later the maintenance men and women in
overalls and stiff aprons polish the table top

and nothing's left there
though borders have been drawn

and lines have been altered
miles away in

nearly unpronounceable cities

Crows fly over Van Gogh's field

and his gunshot scatters them

the gunpowder crack that halts visual explosion and
passionate exploration

In honor of that field real
crows have never flown over it since

and the dark clouds remain

though Van Gogh's spirit hovers there
uncertain which way

to go

Ships at sea have submitted to an
uncertain watery element

like a baby clutching to its
mother's breast in a rocking subway

and if the captain is drunk or sober

it barely matters
unless icebergs appear

If we've learned anything at all it's to be
ever vigilant in every circumstance

but the snow-capped mountain
remains the same vigilant or not

Godlessness and love of God may
look the same from an

observer's point of view

A cliff collapses on both
equally

Almost nothing can be said

But in that nothing
resides two worlds apart

reflective of each other the way
a pool reflects sky

Each of our deaths is totally unique

The fence that separates life from death
is constantly being breached

or hung with strings of electric lights

though the wind batters the boards
equally and finally

tears them to splinters

while God
stays the same

I've seen our cat pounce on nothing at all
with full attention

and wondered who's the fool
the watcher or the watched

though none's the wiser
and a moment later

she's curled up asleep

12/30

OBTRUSION

*"I notice how God keeps obtruding into
your poems"*

"And would you have the world like a
soap bubble instead

just a translucent nothingness that
bursts upon contact with anything that

obstructs it? Or would you prefer
consciousness to obtrude within it

giving it life and radiance and even
for something so fragile a bit more

gumption a bit more
substantiality?

You can attribute the miracle of
consciousness to dumb nature if you want

that animates whale thought and
butterfly migration who without that

obtrusion might float as senselessly as
bubbles across a blank bubble universe

into a continuous bubble nothingness

But for me God's mention must obtrude
into my poems and no poem go on

too long without His obtruding

just as my own heart's bubble would
burst without God's constant and Merciful

obtrusion"

12/30

WET BLACK NOSE

Sky of a yellow dog
the horseman on his huge gray horse

slouched across low sere hills into a
bronze-ish sunset out of town

heading south

The night was a tall black marble that had been
rolled on top of the mountains

He might have been a cowboy or a
Russian Prince who'd just been

spoken to by a bear about things
deeper than he was used to hearing

but he rode with a dejection that had
honky-tonk piano sadness about it

and a little rattlesnake attitude
(whatever that might be)

The marble rolled a little and
clouds appeared across the

cold cold moon

He had a letter in his pocket in a

precise and classical handwriting

instructing the recipient to bring him in and
care for his wounded body and soul

*(I'm thinking cowboy more than Russian Prince
to move the bear story along but*

*it may also have been neither
as we haven't got a description of*

*him or what he's wearing
but to our great surprise he's*

*dressed as a monk
and in fact has*

*furry claws for feet and
a wet black nose)*

                                                  12/30

FOR BETTER OR FOR WORSE

We usually remember people better or
worse than they are

and if they've died
better or worse than they were

while we remember ourselves
as reflections on a clear lake surface

with fluctuating shadows and dappled light
plus a few clouds and sunbursts

which all point to the
infrangibility of the soul as well as its

evanescence and
curious invincibility while incarnated in our

basically fraudulent bodies with their
good-natured smiles and occasional

tantrums causing mirror
reactions by all around us who've now made

indelible memories of their own about
us in all this shimmering mayhem

While what is unchangeable like
the Matterhorn's peak in every

blizzard or blast of solar rays
stays the same

that thing some climb
to achieve the absolute in unfluctuating

height while all the time that
climb and that mountaineer's

majestic victory
resided deep in our selves' plain souls

all along

                                                    12/31

SIREN AT NIGHT

Why is it a siren at night sounds like
someone crying for help

or maybe despairing of help?

Why is it the city at night is like a
single person with disturbed sleep

generally peaceful but now and then
thrashing side to side

and yelling out
under imponderable stars?

Tonight perhaps one person in this entire city's made the
permanent breakthrough into an undying

spectacular radiance that would
light up any number of national

wonders like the Grand Tetons or even
New York itself

yet no one might know of it
but his caged bird or his

insouciant cat
curled up asleep under the Chair of Epiphany

in the roofless room of the
Divine Presence

whose doors and windows have
exploded with light

Now there's another siren across town
speeding to its dutiful appointment

and I pray for safe outcome
surrounded by voices of

sweet council and high jubilation
and the newly ascended saint might also

be hearing it with me and be
flying to the scene in the Unseen

to see by God's pure Seeing
what should be done

and by no action of his own

does it

LOVE FLEW BY THE WINDOW

Love flew by the window
and he almost fell out trying to

catch it

It was a clear blue sky
little planes crisscrossing

a day like any other

Church steeples and high rises
sparrow-clusters festooning the trees

around town

Choir practice going on
some on some off key

Land of sweet liberty!

He saw lava flowing from the sky
his own passions pouring

Everything for a moment
turned golden

People's chatter on the esplanades below
became aphorisms of wisdom

"How much did you pay for it?"
"Everything I had!"

Heart-words everywhere

A taxi letting people out
was a mother letting her children go

but keeping her engine running

He reached for a cloud that
burst full of light

The sky reversed itself and
he became sky

Would I have remained on the
inside? *Did he?*

We conjure
reasons to

love or not to love

and wonder

if we'll drink from its cup
in this life or the

next

The sky turned purple and
drew him in

Every passing bird caught fire
as it flew into his soul

He knew everything had changed
his window looking out on the world

was his window looking in

when love flew by

                                        1/2

CLEAR PERSPECTIVE

It's hard to get a clear perspective say
from the bottom of the

sea with those darling seahorses curling their
tails around your beard and

vibrating in the water those delicate
horse snouts quivering and

bubble streams rising

It's equally difficult to get a proper
beam on a situation from say

a few thousand miles off in
space fixing the capsule with a

lugnut wrench you can't let
go of or it might form a sad

orbit of its own among space-seas of
odds and ends around the

earth rotating like clockwork

Both extremes would gain us nothing if the
heart's eye not be open

and thousands of frightened animals are

pressed up against its gates

The eye of wisdom within every
solitary thing

going on an outing among dour cypress trees
on a gloomy island off Greece

or high atop an Austrian Ferris wheel in the
middle of the night or

crawling with other co-escapees through a
tunnel big enough for

just one body at a time

The heart's eye flutters open like the
nictitating eye of a bird or snake

except the world's other dimension unfurls there
on blue sunny beaches and

silvery sands

And all the faces of all we've known are
here with the

true information of why we were born and
what we're meant to do in the

two or three minutes of our

existence stretched between two bright needles

held apart by God's indivisible

Hands

1/6

TODAY'S THE DAY

On my way here
someone leaned toward me and said

"Today's the day!"

I looked past him at the ribbony
layers of scarlet and gold incandescence

sky was giving birth to above the
jagged city silhouette

hoping for some words in the clouds to
clarify his meaning

I've seen the return of
rectangular soap chicken fricassee and doo-wop

in matching pastel jackets and white hair
days that have gone way by and then

come again

I've seen the return of bison herds though no
near naked braves with bows and

arrows sideways on galloping horses
run them down

And small one stop-sign towns fall into

dust and reemerge as garish

shopping malls

but I'm not sure if
today's the day for them or only a

semblance however hard their
neons blink over and over in the

black night

Yet aside from all these definitely
today is the day

unlike any other with great
grandfather clocks at either end of its

cosmic football-field length going into and
out of a green mist from both ends

much like our lives whose
day this is on every

planetary level at once
to the sound of strangely orchestrated

syncopated music played on

wine glass rims and the gurgling bubbles fish make
undersea

canoodling up to the surface
where their momentariness

breaks into song

This day like the feather put in the
cap of a child who's just

learned how to walk
and in ripples of kinetic pride and

self propulsion bursts into laughter
as the world stands up with her or him

and shows its most
glamorous side of all

God's Day

Trees and ermines
diamonds and rocks

strewn unhaphazardly on our paths
from start to finish

forever

1/8

BREAD

> *Aquesta viva fuente, que deseo*
> *En este pan de vida yo la veo*
> *Aunque de noche.*
> — San Juan de la Cruz

Every soul baked bread in the Unseen
using intergalactic ingredients

and a water so fine it more resembled
air baked in a

fire so bright it more resembled
light

whose nourishment reached every
living being on earth every

hod carrier in India going up narrow
planks with a ton of

bricks on their heads every
beaver building its dam of gnawed

tree boughs blocking up glittering streams

and this bread is what savors in our
own mouths from our births to our

deaths and gives all food its particular
flavor

and the very spores of this bread pour
continuously down from heaven to

fertilize crops and fallow fields below

Ancient natives still imbibing it
as their ghost tribes accordian into their

long hills of repose under a green sun

It's manna from heaven for migrating nations
unsure of their direction but whose

taste of patience keeps them from the brink

A backwards baking that connects us in its
industrious energy to the very

vibrational core of every being
ever alive and whose

taste alone brings new beings to life
within this risen miracle of creation

It's the sharp twinkle between stars against a
background of funneling nothingness

in which only the Divine Something
really breathes in every direction at once

a lit entity at the beginning

that meets us at the sweet

moments of our end in even the
direst circumstances

merging into the next world as
easily as it entered into this

Fresh-baked aroma of streams
emanating from its loaf as surely as the

starry waters of heaven
pour everywhere now and forever

One finger in our mouths from having
tested it

One finger in our hearts
from the freshness of its taste

1/14

MOMENTS

A moment came in on a silver platter
ringed around with race horses in full

gallop

Another seemed to be throwing kisses from the
back of a train as it left almost

before it arrived

A particularly golden moment came in High-C
sustained over quite a long

stretch so that the moment took on an
almost gelatinous or elastic quality

One moment seemed to stop dead in its tracks
pulling time before it and time

after it with which it might have
spelled the doom of us all

Things take place in the ample or strict
spaces of moments including this poem

and the agile sitting body you can't see of
its momentary writer

America was discovered in a poignant moment when

one of its original natives really took in

the beauty of a waterfall or the way
sunlight shone on rippling stream pebbles

Wars are won or lost in a slippery moment
inside and beyond or perhaps exactly in inverse

ratio to the silence that all the shouting and
bloodshed accumulates in a very

tumultuous and decisive moment

Waves on distant shores say in Polynesia
seem as if they might be exempt from moments altogether as they

lap deliciously at white sands flecked with
tiny precious stones rolled around in their

froth but in actuality *(though in such serene zones*
even these waves in tiny increments are also particularly

autonomous moments

and both jellyfish and crabs who may be either
running after or being run after know this better than any

impartial viewer standing here
savoring the moment)

all this begins to resemble the assemblage of a

puzzle the very mosaic way all moments

fit together to make up an appearance of
time and reality

though it may be that on slippery silver skis
invisible to our eyes we ourselves are carried

moment by moment to the great momentous
meeting with both our selves and our Lord

Who of all things is truly free of the moment as well as
its supreme Arbiter and Measurer in

entire galaxies of the Endless Moment above all

moons and suns in their happy
orbits in the flexibly sprung single and

all-pervasive moment each of us witnesses each
moment whether or not we take

note of it as it hovers expectantly between
arriving and departing like the

gleam on a soap bubble or the
intensely dwelled-in kiss of a beloved say

at the top loop of a roller coaster before
zooming down the greatest dip in the world to the

sound of grinding wheels and suddenly
shocked and strangely suspended

shouts of joy
held

momentously

in the

moment

1/16

MOTHER TIME

Ruthless and unrelenting
time picks off of us *(with a certain*

tenderness the way a mother might remove
splinters one at a time or

bits of broken glass where we fell)

time picks off of us a bit here a bit there
a little eyesight here a little hearing there or

a stiff joint here or there
so slowly we

might not even notice it except that
flake by flake or ache by ache

we do

But she *(I'm making Time feminine to*
even the score perhaps the way

hurricanes were double gendered at last)

has the tenderest of intentions since she may be
doing these things to us while right outside the

window a nest of baby birds breaks into
hungry cheeping and new ferns uncurl their

feathery tips

Time so tender for the most part but
not always

Unrelenting without question and as
ruthless in her way as a runaway train

steaming off a cliff

Allah says *"Do not curse Time for*
Time IS Allah"

and I go back to trying to
understand this hadith koan

It's not just God the Victor over our
lives at the end of the game with

grim pinball lights mockingly flashing

but that we befriend time alongside
our increasing blindness or deafness

making each one a kind of animal rescue
like seals from the sea found

battered and bitten but put in
cool pools to end their days out of

the mammalian

rat race of jeopardy

Great old mother Time
despite her gentle touch

her modern remedies
her ancient poultices

pat by pat and soothing smoothness
by soothing smoothness

that in the end no longer
quite cure

Time the so much stronger
the so much

more Pure

                                                          1/17

DANCING ON THE HEAD OF A PIN

Perhaps the bear doesn't see the angel at first
or perhaps the bear imagines the angel so

vividly the angel appears
casting no shadow

How the bear or how
I myself got in the cage or

how the Prince became the bear
is beyond me at this moment's

contemplation
though truly nothing

is or should be

It's an imperceptible sponging up of
one into the other

moment into contemplation
contemplation into moment

How else do we find ourselves in the
predicament of being anyone at all?

If we squint we see a blank wall
but the bear with those tiny and

none-too acute eyes squints and sees
(God bless it) angels

Can it be blamed for bettering its
vision and literally

giving it wings?

If you stand in a waterfall
everything's blurred but the very

divine crash of water is so
sublime a thing what's

blurred becomes a trembling cause for
wonder

All blank walls have tiny etchings in them
made there by hands doing God's bidding each

etching of which somehow
echoes the whole out to the

raggedy edges of the stars

The Prince speaks through the bear and the
bear speaks though the Prince

and we glance quickly and see a
corridor through the trees to escape the

claustrophobic self and go where
wings congregate and a

flutter of light ascending around and
through us lifts the gates of our

watery eyes

Oh this is the time of a dancing bear!

*This is the time of angels
dancing*

on the head of a pin!

1/27

THE MOST TANGIBLE SONGS OF OUR HEARTS

Love broke down and cried
then swept its pieces into a

vase into which it placed the long-stemmed
object of its quest

that continues to open its blooms petal by
petal until stars are

caught in its rosy extensions

No window gazed out of nor even a
casual glance cast out of does not contain

love's wonders with
every last intentional bee meandered

past on its own sweet quest or high flock of
geese honking along in upper atmospheres

automatically heading for more
inclement weather

Then there's the elegant Victorian drawing room
version with its initial flirtation then

intriguing middle section with or without
children and stuttering housemaids and a

tragedy or two

Then a long sigh in place of a neat
dénouement with a slow diminishment of the

cast of characters and memory's eye looking back at
the signs and shadows of love's impact

and the heart's really ageless nostalgia
a place where panthers play like cats

and a certain haunting music repeats itself
over and over

under a flowering cherry tree

Love comes in on a white horse
and out on a black one

or vice versa

and no corridor of bending cypresses
quite covers both its entrances and exits

And each sunset is itself the golden
buttons on love's coat as it

buttons up for the long gallop into eternity

love's main thoroughfare
where saints appear in the Beloved's glow

waving in that incredibly friendly way saints have
or with flicks of their eyes communicate

the epic love poem we are all so earnestly
learning to write

inexhaustible in its variations
though purified and tempered by them

beyond every morality known

Oh love
like the Face of God

you and death the true subjects of all our
most fruitful outpourings

We the lone harpist in a resonant courtyard
calling out to appear in all its

arched windows at once

love's countenance
bending into view

as our harp's echoes ricochet upward
along rough bricks then burst in

free pyrotechnics to the stars

If we heard our own voices calling you

they might resemble to us the

gauche squawks of irascible swans

but let them be to your ears

Oh love Oh God Oh death in your
multiple disguises

the most tangible
songs of our hearts

                                                                    1/30

THE RADICAL FORMATION OF THINGS

The radical formation of things
met the sublimely Zen-like everydayness of things

in a neutral zone in some nameless dimension

and both agreed it didn't have to be
spectacular and tremendous like the

deep-in-the-bowels of the earth
crushing of diamonds over eons

but also say a kind of nonchalant
tossed-off kind of thing like an

ant carrying a crumb across a sink
or an exhaust cloud puffing out a car's

exhaust pipe into the air

Not just revolution in the streets with
millions of Egyptians all waking up at once

filling street corridors between buildings with
resonant slogans forged in the

operatic workshops of heaven

but also a calm conversation between two
Italian taxi drivers sitting on their cab-hoods on a

slow day outside a train station

All and both extravagant and simple in every case cut out of
divine enchantment propelled by

God's breath recognized as such or not
as momentous in suchness as

a dramatic rescue at sea with
multiple helicopters and a massive

circling of whales

or that ant finally getting that
crumb to safety somewhere to

chomp on it in complete contentment

Everything echoing great valleys of angelic hallelujahs
ricocheting back and forth across

cloudless heavens
and just as blandly and matter-of-factly

being someone somewhere rocking in a rocking chair
musing on nothing eyes wide open or closed

as eternity with all its vivid pictures
in riotous colors or in softer pastel hues

gallops or whispers through us

maintaining its mystery or its no-frills

simplicity in the godly cavalcade and
occasional shooting gallery of this world

where everything is something and
often somethings turn out to be

nothing at all

but all have resonant meanings
wrapped in extravagant garb

or in quiet thrift store hand-me-downs
catching in their compass

all earth's and sky's
pristine available light

SPAGHETTI NOODLES

Spaghetti noodles no longer resemble the brain
nor do half walnuts

Nothing resembles what it
started out to be

The brain could be called a luminous ship
crossing ghostly oceans on the

lookout not only for white whales and
inhabited isles but also

the cure for cancer and some very
intractable mathematical equations

but not cooked spaghetti noodles
in a bowl

At the same time the bowl of heaven with its
radiant rotating bodies might

resemble the brain

Do stars call out to each other
across space?

Does a giant horse really leap from
one galaxy to another with the

greatest of ease?

If we sit very still and squinch our eyes
or better still gently close them

are we suddenly spatial neighbors with
some distant celestial configurations

now made near?

Our beings have both original and
ultimate transparency

In some ways we can resemble anything
the River Nile say on a sunny day

or an inaccessible gorge somewhere in the
Tyrolean Alps

or the tiniest mosquito looking for dinner
or the satisfied lion having found it

Sitting across from God at the same table
can be very instructive

And I say this knowing that my image of Him
endemically falls utterly short no matter how

theologically careful I might be

Sitting across from everything is always

potentially instructive if we carefully

open our given sensorium to let in
starlight

Having been born
looking at nothing at all

can be instructive

But if we sit ourselves across from God
we're bound to see and hear things

never before conceived in the brain of man
however noodly

I want to get out of here and
into here at the same time

Cross all space on that leaping horse
and diminish to gnat-size or smaller

But the ongoing twenty-four hour love that
keeps us in these bodes day after day

is what seats us across from God in His
invisibility

and through these eyes He's given us
we can watch His spectral and less

spectral movements and hear the
elegant *whoosh* of His ways

as close to us as we are

as far away as the stars

2/7

THE KING BECAME HIS BREAKFAST

The king became his breakfast that he ate
as he ate it

so delicious were its tidbits its glacés its
sherbets and its fruits

The horse became the air it jumped through
as it jumped the bush

and when it landed became the horse again
it always was

The shrill boat whistle became all the
ears that heard it far and

near and when it ceased
ears reattached themselves to heads

heads to necks and continued
on their way

The way became each one who went
on it one by one and

all at once just as nothing
becomes us all and then we're

something again rare and strange
in another world than this one

which has become itself again
with others in it

and the siren sound and rooster crow
and sky clouds cross in

become all of us and none of us
and God is God Who's never become

any of these things and all these
incorporeal things at once

A smile across our faces when the
wind blows

A hurricane across the earth
as we go

into its greater smile
that better becomes us

after all

2/12

RADIANCE OF HORSES

for Salihah & Douglas

A radiance of horses sweeping from a
point of invisibility on an endless plain

It might have been herds of bison or
glittering marching bands

great juggernaut processions filling space
or jinn whirlwinds from the Unseen in a

panic to fulfill an impossible pledge

low flying Monarch butterflies clustered together
on their annual migration

or people's thoughts
out for a spin across emptiness before

entering emptiness again at the other end

But it's a radiance of horses
in synchronous waves with sunlight

greasing their moist muscular pulses
sleeker than thought is

burst in the distance from a
point of invisibility heading from

right to left across the visible field
wild atoms in a rainbow

planets pouring across space in the
trajectory of a single flash of spatial silver

almost gone before it appears
quicker than the ignition of force at the

source of the Nile
glad band of elements in a

devotional mass moving slower than nightfall
in a wink so fast they're almost entirely missed

This radiance of horses

heart-stopping explosion

from a point in invisibility to

God's own infinite spaces

that love is

2/17

IT'S TOO LATE TO SAVE THE PATIENT

It's too late to save the patient
he mostly extends out

on the other side

His eyes are open and his weak voice
articulates

but it's to late to save the patient

Patchworks of hills and hamlets
roll into the sky

Livestock moo hens cackle
weeping women look down at him

but it's too late to save the patient

Someone's pulling the heavens over to
cover him

Stars blink out their influential
configurations

but it's too late to save the patient

Sons and daughter gather from
far and wide

The saucer-eyed and grim ones some with their
own children

but it's too late to save the patient

His good is already going on display
his bad lurks ready to spring

A veil of mercy slowly filters down

but it's too late to save the patient

His hair grows over this world like a cloud
one micrometer at a time

but never entirely covers it

His fingertips miles from
anything tangible

His feet not touching solid floor
for weeks

His heart beats softly on this side
but more and more on the other side

sounding like chimes there rather than
muffled throbs

All possible upheavals in the world don't
affect him now next to this one

All its avalanches stop dead in their tracks
their muddy hands up to their muddy mouths

All the oceans for a moment
grow still

very still

2/18

THERE IS NO DISTANCE

"There is this distance between me and what I see"
— Philip Lamantia

There is no distance between us and
what we see

Is this the fields of Paradise?
Is this God's running place?

How can it be otherwise?
Fluted columns of light support the heavens

Space is crowded with bridges to other worlds
where zebras leap out of the cages of their

stripes into savannas of light
but in *this* world

right before our noses
the ones that grow hairs out their nostrils

and mosquitoes land on to sting

Two radiant people marry in a hospital room
and the world changes color to various

shades of turquoise
before becoming again its normal vivid self

though no one remains quite the same
and I'm looking out a window where

night herons cawing are heading across a lagoon
and egrets land noisily on cypress branches

batting out their pecking order for sleep

"Turn away from this world" they say
"and you will see God"

*"Turn away from God
and you will see the world"*

I say *"Turn away from God
and you will still see God"*

standing and sitting and reclining on
your side

Nothing impedes us but
impediment itself

from looking down into the technicolor
checkerboard of our hearts born out of

flesh and blood's passionate heat
to melt snow on a mountaintop

in the devotional heat of the sun
where zebras still run

and only a lion whose mane is a crown
can catch them

*Are these all just abstractions to
hold in the mind?*

If we look deep into a cesspool's murk
do we see God's Face?

And what's that Face so lively but no
human features?

What's that Smile of uttermost Benevolence

without lips that curve like the most

lithe and graceful of bows whose arrows
pierce us to our cores?

A silver man on a silver stallion
rides through the blue world before it

turns back to its usual hues

His song scintillates the wind twitch of grasses and
inaudible chimes at the

center of the earth
whose louvers suddenly open to reveal

the black bird of marriage turning equally

silver in the very things we see
in the very spaces they reside in

in all the spatial
randomness of their placements and displacements

where each face is the faces of this couple
obliterated in the Face of God

beaming at us over the sunrising
horizon at the very ends of our fingertips

as a surgeon snips off a stomach polyp in an
overlit room beeping with computers

as a wet nurse runs out of a burning house
saving only five babies out of twelve

as tanks rumble across a
blood-spattered square using usury's gasoline

that the zebra freed from its zigzag cage
crosses in a single bound

"You can't see in the dark" you say
"You can't see in the light" some say

The heart's vision clear
in every climate

The space between me

and what I see

God's space

in every case

                                        2/22
                                 (Lankanau Hospital)

HIS TIGHT EMBRACE

Allah has us in His tight embrace
It's a thrill to know this!

And that His Hands reach right through us
to massage a delicate interior place

unseen or unfelt by us but known to Him
better than any microscope can tell

He's there after the end
and before the beginnings of all things

in time and space as well as in
no time and no space all

held in His tight embrace
in which we dwell

2/24

SOME DEATHS

He died filing his nails

She died blowing kisses to angels through a
round window

He died in a chair reading a book and
reaching the Ultimate Knowledge

She died sitting on a rock contemplating
her garden

He died on steep steps having just written his
Ode to Machu Picchu

She died after adjusting the last family photo
into its frame

He died dipping his airplane wings over the
twinkling lights of Oakland

She died having finally sighted an albino giraffe

He died underwater having discovered the
tumbled pillars of Atlantis

She died in space peacefully circling Mars

He died happily pushing celery stalks into
a juicer

She died on a slow boat to China
in her dreams

And the golden casket from which flow
all the decrees of these deaths and

every other on earth

shines like the Holy Grail in purest resplendence
even for deaths that seem

commonplace in the telling

though the death of no sparrow goes
unrecognized

nor that of a tiny ant on its endless quest
ambitiously along a sink

searching everywhere for the

Beneficent
Face of God

2/24

TALE OF TEN DOCTORS AND A SNOWMAN

Ten doctors go into a yard to diagnose a
snowman

The first doctor notes the anemic condition of
its skin as it

glistens in the light which he says is due to
a lack of exercise and red meat

The second doctor notes the carbonization of
its eyes that can't seem to

focus and says that too much heat has
impaired their visual range and he should

cool them down with ice packs

The third doctor notes its carrot nose and says
its appearance so contrasts with the

rest of its body that a rare form of
proto-vegetal vestigial proboscisnosis is

endangering the rest of its extremities and
orders it julienned or at least

slivered into curly fronds

The fourth doctor notes its total lack of

internal organs and predicts dire consequences and

puts it on a regime of organ donorship in which
all natural organs can be somehow

inserted and activated immediately

The fifth doctor takes note of its hands that are
woolen gloves on sticks and suggests it has

come by this living too close to a sweater factory
and a kind of paralysis has affected its

fingers to such an extent a physical therapist
should be called in to try to work its

fuzzy fingers into greater flexibility

The sixth doctor exclaims the rotundity of its
lower body is due to an internal bloating no doubt caused by

extreme consumption of cold to nearly freezing
liquid and puts it on a solid diet of

hot peppers and strong coffee

The seventh doctor is gravely concerned about its
total lack of legs and notes it is

suffering from a kind of elephantiasis especially around the
knees which have virtually disappeared

and calls on a team of surgeons to attempt to
correct its tragic abnormality with little

hope for success

The eighth doctor notes the molecular transparency of its
bodily structure and suggests a complete

plastic surgery makeover gradually replacing its
main trunk with one made of a specially

formulated polyurethane sheathing

The ninth doctor stands back and surveys
how quickly its general obesity has shrunk to an

anorexic skeletal appearance and
orders a diet of massive carbohydrates and

huge amounts of synthetic protein to try to
fatten it up as fast as possible

The tenth doctor peers at it and
stutters and stammers with his

stethoscope held suspended in the air
wavering there

because the snowman has by now
melted

entirely away

                              2/24
                       (Lankanau Hospital)

SAINT JOHN OF THE CROSS IN PRISON

Saint John of the Cross stood up in his
prison cell and its stones became

donuts

He knew this was from the devil so he
did not eat

He knew that if he ate his state would go dark
the radiant escalators of his

innermost sunlight would vanish
the skies of black brilliance in which he

dwelt showered by God direct would
congeal into a sodden cloud

He turned and glanced out the
shimmering licorice bars of the window onto

vague milky daylight and
swallowed his dry swallow in which

the fresh cascades of Andalusia
splashed refreshingly into his heart

He sat down again this time on his
hard bed which by Divine Grace had become

a donkey riding him across green
mountainsides aglitter with sparrows

above the churning sea of God's Good Pleasure
crashing against the

rocks of his heartbeats below

2/26

DESTINY INSIDE-OUT

1

Destiny's more than the name of a horse or a
stripper —

Like the weather according to Mark Twain
"Everybody talks about it but

no one does anything about it"
And what pray tell *can* we do?

Destiny digs in like skate blades on a pond
sometimes even making that

same scraping noise

Engineers try to bypass or at least
accommodate destiny by building their

bridges and buildings with pre-stressed
materials to withstand earthquakes or

great aerial impacts

but that's really just like tying our
shoes nice and tight before taking a

long walk and Destiny itself

has no particular fondness or aversion to
shoes or feet or any of the

sartorial accoutrements we might don before
heading out into

Destiny's high crosswinds

It's a sudden hole in a wall that lets us through
or a sudden wall in a hole that

stops us

Its very sweet music tumbles together
events and eventualities like precision

tumblers in a combination safe or those famous
puzzle pieces that look abstract at first

but when assembled properly show
Abraham Lincoln all stiff and white sitting in his

great marble chair in Washington DC a prime
example of how Destiny works in our

favor but often uses what seems to us like
crude means to do so

Lincoln now rather sainted sitting perhaps in
one of the lofty balconies in

Paradise this very moment discussing his near-fabled life with
Shakespeare

Destiny has its own wheels though we might try to
put wheels on it ourselves to either

meet it head on or avert it altogether speeding on
past it to Las Vegas and wild nights of

irresponsible gambling

Underwater meetings with Destiny and
midair encounters always have a

particular poignancy though Destiny doesn't always
entail death but maybe only

the death of one thing or direction and the
birth of another by complete surprise

or the slow nod of recognition of
its certain inevitabilities

and I haven't even yet mentioned Destiny's great
Captain the always inspired

Chess Master spontaneously making His

absolute moves as well as
extending the chessboard itself out in

all directions at once
that neither man nor computer can

outwit or out-move *O may the minions who*
carry out His directives to our lives

always glisten the air with their silvery wings
and continue to transmit back to Him

in their melodious voices
our supplications for comfortable turns of

events and glowing chapels of
convivial jubilations *amen*

We continue to pray and
He never stops moving for even one nanosecond

and what seemed arbitrary years ago
might in the next moment's machinations turn out

to make perfect and blesséd sense with

pinball machine music of its happy clappers and its
flashing lights illuminating that

rainy street in Paris we went down in
1982 or that

person we met whose card we just
found again in a tatty coat pocket

It's really an inexhaustible subject after all
the lithe perfectly choreographed and

synchronized dancers of
Destiny in their mythical masks and

sonorous voices always doing their thing both
before and within us

It's forever ready and ripe enough to eat
or glisteningly raw right off the tree

like the infamous apple and that first bite that
changed everything forever

But redemption both in it and through it might entail

burrowing straight into it head first
with a happy enough face on and our

hearts galloping towards it like sleek horses and
as naked as strippers

for in fact in all its possible horrors and
seemingly tragic inaccuracies such as

"bad things happen to good people"
Destiny's clocks are all set to the

same time in the same space at once
and its mechanisms when viewed with as

godly eyes as possible though never matching
God's Eyes themselves *(may they be*

a billion times blessed upon
themselves and within themselves)

when we wash the lenses clean of our
own eyes' orbs both innermost and outermost

we see great illumined girders sliding into place
with *yes yes yes* and *yes again* perfectly intelligent design

to make such a holy mandala after all such a
gloriously assembled syntax of obvious

meaning whose all bells ring and
whose chimes sing such harmonious scales

we're left panting and weeping all at the same time

the picture that emerges is the
total immersion and consubstantiation of

ourselves within it
that we can't see where

we end and Destiny begins at the very
tender moment of its uncanny unlocking of us

— *Oh dear horse and dear stripper of us named*
Destiny after all!

2

Oh God I
bless You and praise You with a

love that's beyond me to
express that's Yours anyway

standing here looking back at my
life at this moment seeing

how perfectly it's been arranged

that if there's even one
single hair out of place

You comb it with Your

big comb

2/27

THE BLIND NIGHT WATCHMAN

I'd always stood at the side door
waiting for the little blind night watchman

(chosen because of his innate similarity with the night)
to make his rounds

though he couldn't see the splattering of
stars above the silhouette ramparts

those tiny lenses above us beaming down from the
first workshop

I'd always waited in shadows
hoping they'd cover me with their

fuzzy gabardines

to let splendors pass me like
golden coaches filled with royal

families pulled by giant bison low to the
ground moving slowly enough for me to

contemplate all the gilded angelic carvings
everywhere resplendent on their sides

Occasionally a caparisoned charger would
go by followed by twelve stealthy panthers

almost invisible in the blackness except for their
eye beams and I would step out from the

waiting door to get a better look
shrinking back again

hoping they hadn't
noticed me

as they passed

Night and its wonders!
Processions and confabulations!

Its arena filled to the top with
God's trapezes as well as the

nonsensical bustle of His earthier clowns

But one moment pricked by a splinter
and it all flashed past with a kind of

subtle incandescence making things
day bright

the world's everything indistinguishable in
its shimmering silk stretched from

horizon to horizon though I could still spy
stars at the very top

pouring down their tart liquors

I squint to see figures emerge from it
the way I could make out

even the king's elephants from
night's murk

I tell my heartbeats to hammer on the door of
light and dark's Engineer

whose pulses I feel throbbing in my
neck as His brightness envelopes me

in His greater Gaze
in the night's quiet

as the blind night watchman comes and goes

tapping out his
circular rounds

2/27

OFFSHOOTS

> *God Appears & God is Light*
> *to those poor Souls who dwell in Night*
> *But does a Human Form Display*
> *To those who dwell in Realms of Day*
>   — William Blake

We're offshoots from the main branch
or rather offshoots of offshoots of offshoots

back down to the original couple God made
make us up the line unbeknownst

to them at the time

If we pull the camera back what
do we see?

A tree? A growing incrementally
offshoot by offshoot extending spiral of

incredible leafiness going twitchingly
round and round in a dark mauve

sunlight?

But we're simply somewhere on the
branchings ourselves as the

spiral corkscrews ghostly past us to
further selves we

can't conceive of though we
may have conceived them

So if we pull back the camera even
further in this yodeling upward

rainfall of genetic confabulation each
new nodule waving at us as if to

invite us over for a bite even though nearly or
precisely prehistoric or so far in the

future we're no longer sure which
planet we're living on by then

If we pull back the camera even
further *Praise the Lord* are we part of a

slowly spiraling constellation wearing
stars in its hair as

God turns the spiral by His sweet Will and
Determination though no matter how

far back we pull the camera
we may not see Him?

Glory to His clear concentration as each new
spiraling twitch smooth as glass

produces more and more of us to

infinity

wearing stars in our hair each
heart-beating consciousness of each one of us

conceiving of cosmos both as wide or
wider than the visible heavens as well as

so small as to include all newborns
just now being pushed into

daylight by their mothers still
asweat on their birth-beds

Whole pictorial and aural cosmologies down to
excruciatingly precise detail such as the

names and birth dates as well as
every relationship ever to be

encountered in a lifespan outward as well as
simultaneously inward

wearing stars in our hair
our segment part of this glittering

matchstick structure in space
spiraling away forever put into

motion at some point and at some point
destined to come to a stop

The song or cry in the night of it
even right now

audible in our throats in its deep
pure melody in our hearts

2/28

THE KNOCKING

> "... all that remained to him of
> life, after that time, caused him joy!"
> — St. John of the Cross / *Living Flame of Love*

I've got a lot of information coming in
from the depot at the edge of the

desert

where Sancho's donkey stands by a
dry well while

Don Quixote's swaybacked nag nibbles
non-existent grass

And the sky's part of it with its
clouds cut out of the blue

like fluffy windows looking at the
void and describing tropical abundance

lush vegetation with entwining vines
entering deepest caves and bringing out

exiled angels ready to repent of their
insubordinations that went against

no one but their own selves' soft feathers and pale
silken wings

The sand is full of footprints going
every which way yet

no one's ever come here at least
no one with feet

Papers float along hot low-lying winds

I snatch them out of the air and
put them through a little

translation device made of spider web gossamer
the machinery of sunken ships and

an orchestra of grasshoppers
sawing away with their

violinic back legs

This just came to me without
any inducements

Some of it useful
some of it mysteriously as useless as

nipples on a man

But afar off there may just be a
cargo-laden ship docking fresh from the blackest

sky at the depot

and a crew of *a cappella* spirits singing as they

pull ropes and swab decks

loud enough for me to hear
across the sandy wastes

to the side of my bed in Philadelphia where I
write this

"It all began" he said leaning back against a rock
"when I was a child

and a rhinoceros would
snort outside my window

maybe not a tree full of angels as there
was for young William Blake

but these days the memory of those sonorous
rhinoceros songs sorts out the

words from the melodies slow enough for me to
write them down word for word

in more melodious tones"

A gas station would look good over there
or a Ferris wheel

Sounds of excited children would

alleviate the dry silence of the desert that

only accommodates
tiny crinkles like the crab-crawls of scorpions

with occasional howls at a full moon
or the roars of sandstorms

Each word as precise as a sword slice
into a bag full of water

Each image floating past these dry eyes
an excuse for grand pronouncements and

minute descriptions of barely existent realities

as we all are

Oh I knocked on God's door once
and the sound of my knocking has

never ceased knocking to this day

It sustains me through the cold nights

that same knock knocked and
still knocking

so long ago

3/1

PASTORAL

Sheep look to their shepherd
for grassy knolls

protection from wolves
a night covered with stars

but with a certain
skittishness that the

shepherd might eat them

Fish in their schools
look to their sisters and

brothers to move through the deeps in
symbiotic harmony as graceful as

silk cloth shifting in wind
watching out their two eyes to

move as one
for graceful solidarity

Ants have a job to do
and do it with precision having

nearly landed on their feet from
birth to do so

without any formal education

looking to their Queen though she be
hidden from sight

prolifically producing out of herself
her brood of immaculate servants

Flowers look to the sky from their roots
and push up through dirt to reach it

and though it's always beyond their
grasp bloom tiny or extravagant

often odorous clusters
freely offering their pollen in

God's interactive circular scheme

since bees and butterflies
look to them ever-restlessly

seeking out both their
hidden and more obvious beauties

The lion looks to his Lord
himself lord of the earthly

gazing with regal gazes
with a calm that

conceals his nearly indefatigable
strength until he

comes to an elephant

gargantuan implacable
looking to the world for just the

tons of vegetation it needs daily
more akin to whales in their

search for krill gliding through
dark with sagacious eyes

giants who actually speak with a
precise vocabulary whose

eloquence breathed by God Himself
if we could only hear it and understand it

would bring us to tears

3/2

LAST WISH

I can imagine the last wish of someone
gazing at death being

driving down to the Jersey Shore to one of those
egg breakfast restaurants you have to

wait outside with everyone for about
an hour before getting a table then

you get one over to the side a booth and
the place is packed with people families with

multiple children some crying some
running around and you wait for about

fifteen minutes for a waitress to get your
order and she goes away having

forgotten your water and you begin to
notice the old couple next to you or

a few tables away out on the floor
probably not tourists bur residents a

certain quiet solid look about them
and it takes another fifteen minutes for

the glasses of water and two mugs of weak coffee
to come I'm with my wife and we chat about

this and that or try to remember a
movie we saw we both liked

and there's a huge hubbub and laughing soon
of a family reunion or something one long

table with people coming in in small groups
hugging and sitting down and still

laughing and suddenly a little boy with a
toy truck runs past and his young

mother with blond ponytail runs
after him

and in the background you realize is music
bland orchestrated Beatles songs for restaurants

and the waitress forgot to take the
menus you've looked at a few times for the

last twenty minutes
laminated photos of waffles and short stacks

with or without fried eggs and

a great *whoop* goes up and it's a
birthday breakfast and over there there's

singing and a few wait persons
standing nearby and beaming and then

after another twenty minutes or so as you
notice a fire truck rumbling by outside

the window without its siren blaring and another
huge line of people waiting to get in

the waitress brings your food

3/5

A STOPPERED BOTTLE

A stoppered bottle holds a genie
but a genie holds the bottle

not knowing that another genie
holds them both in his

long green hands inside a cove of
electric fire

as sand dunes below them all whisper and
shift changing position so we

never know exactly where we've been
or where we're going

Blue sky as blue as the eyes of a
saint who sees all this in his

heart's eye seated in a shaft of
sunlight who then

blows across his right palm and all three
genies disappear

popping up somewhere in far Mongolian Steppes
where an entranced shaman puts them

up his brocaded sleeve for later use as he
gallops across the tundra on his

squat fiery horse seeing
landscapes of the heavens in his

wild eyes and kisses the Beloved of us all
with pursed lips

3/6

INDEX

A Stoppered Bottle   196
Author's Foreword   6
Black Top White Top   24
Black and Silver Angel   56
Bony Horse   37
Bread   127
Cat Pounce   105
Clear Perspective   121
Dancing on the Head of a Pin   137
Destiny Inside-Out   172
Don Quixote   11
Doors   89
Duck's Back   33
Facing Inward   99
For Better or For Worse   114
Grit   78
His Tight Embrace   163
Hitting Bulls Eye   58
Houses Turn into House-Shaped Dust   19
How if We Haven't Left   42
I Haven't Said Anything Yet   91
I Heard the Angels   53
If We Had a Choice   44
Inscriptions Among Ruins   47
It's Too Late to Save The Patient   155
I'm Sailing Inward   84
Ladder Leaned up Against the House   80
Last Wish   193
Lord of Introspection   60
Love Flew by the Window   118
Moments   130
Mother Time   134
Multiplications and Subtractions   95

Night Begins Early   39
Obtrusion   110
Offshoots   182
Pastoral   190
Radiance of Horses   153
Saint John of the Cross in Prison   170
Seeking Sweetness   15
Single Contemplation   82
Siren at Night   116
Snow Deer   93
So Little Effort   50
Some Deaths   164
Sometimes Going to Sleep is Strange   17
Spaghetti Noodles   147
Table   30
Tale of the Ten Doctors and a Snowman   166
The Bear Narrative 2   97
The Bear Narrative   64
The Blind Night Watchman   179
The Color of The Lord   14
The Dark More Golden   21
The King Became His Breakfast   151
The Knocking   186
The Light and the Dark of It   49
The Luster of a Glisten   26
The Most Tangible Songs of Our Hearts   140
The Only Sound She Hears   28
The Radical Formation of Things   144
The Shattering   86
There is No Distance   158
Today's the Day   124
We Should All Be Very Happy   101
Wet Black Nose   112
When the Portal Opened   35

ABOUT THE AUTHOR

Born in 1940 in Oakland, California, Daniel Abdal-Hayy Moore's first book of poems, *Dawn Visions*, was published by Lawrence Ferlinghetti of City Lights Books, San Francisco, in 1964, and the second in 1972, *Burnt Heart/Ode to the War Dead*. He created and directed *The Floating Lotus Magic Opera Company* in Berkeley, California in the late 60s, and presented two major productions, *The Walls Are Running Blood*, and *Bliss Apocalypse*. He became a Sufi Muslim in 1970, performed the Hajj in 1972, and lived and traveled throughout Morocco, Spain, Algeria and Nigeria, landing in California and publishing *The Desert is the Only Way Out*, and *Chronicles of Akhira* in the early 80s (Zilzal Press). Residing in Philadelphia since 1990, in 1996 he published *The Ramadan Sonnets* (Jusoor/City Lights), and in 2002, *The Blind Beekeeper* (Jusoor/Syracuse University Press). He has been the major editor for a number of works, including *The Burdah* of Shaykh Busiri, translated by Hamza Yusuf, and the poetry of Palestinian poet, Mahmoud Darwish, translated by Munir Akash. He is also widely published on the worldwide web: *The American Muslim, DeenPort*, and his own website and poetry blog, among others: *www.danielmoorepoetry.com, www.ecstaticxchange.wordpress.com*. He has been poetry editor for *Seasons Journal, Islamica Magazine*, a 2010 translation by Munir Akash of *State of Siege*, by Mahmoud Darwish (Syracuse University Press), and *The Prayer of the Oppressed*, by Imam Muhammad Nasir al-Dar'i, translated by Hamza Yusuf. In 2011 he was a winner of the Nazim Hikmet Prize for Poetry. *The Ecstatic Exchange Series* is bringing out the extensive body of his works of poetry (a complete list of published works on page 2).

POETIC WORKS by Daniel Abdal-Hayy Moore
Published and Unpublished

Dawn Visions (published by City Lights, 1964)
Burnt Heart/Ode to the War Dead (published by City Lights, 1972)
This Body of Black Light Gone Through the Diamond (printed by Fred Stone, Cambridge, Mass, 1965)
On The Streets at Night Alone (1965?)
All Hail the Surgical Lamp (1967)
States of Amazement (1970)

Abdallah Jones and the Disappearing-Dust Caper (published by The Ecstatic Exchange/Crescent Series, 2006)
'Ala ud-Deen and the Magic Lamp
The Chronicles of Akhira (1981) (published by Zilzal Press with Typoglyphs by Karl Kempton, 1986; published in Sparrow on the Prophet's Tomb by The Ecstatic Exchange, 2009)
Mouloud (1984) (A Zilzal Press chapbook, 1995; published in Sparrow on the Prophet's Tomb by The Ecstatic Exchange, 2009)
Man is the Crown of Creation (1984)
The Look of the Lion (The Parabolas of Sight) (1984)
The Desert is the Only Way Out (completed 4/21/84) (Zilzal Press chapbook, 1985)
Atomic Dance (1984) (am here books, 1988)
Outlandish Tales (1984)
Awake as Never Before (12/26/84) (Zilzal Press chapbook, 1993)
Glorious Intervals (1/1/85) (Zilzal Press chapbook, ?)
Long Days on Earth/Book I (1/28 – 8/30/85)
Long Days on Earth/Book II (Hayy Ibn Yaqzan)
Long Days on Earth/Book III (1/22/86)
Long Days on Earth/Book IV (1986)
The Ramadan Sonnets (Long Days on Earth/Book V) (5/9 – 6/11/86) (published by Jusoor/City Lights Books, 1996) (republished as Ramadan Sonnets by The Ecstatic Exchange, 2005)
Long Days on Earth/Book VI (6-8/30/86)
Holograms (9/4/86 – 3/26/87)
History of the World (The Epic of Man's Survival) (4/7 – 6/18/87)
Exploratory Odes (6/25 – 10/18/87)

The Man at the End of the World (11/11 – 12/10/87)
The Perfect Orchestra (3/30 – 7/25/88)(published by The Ecstatic Exchange, 2009)
Fed from Underground Springs (7/30 – 11/23/88)
Ideas of the Heart (11/27/88 – 5/5/89)
New Poems (scattered poems, out of series, from 3/24 – 8/9/89)
Facing Mecca (5/16 – 11/11/89)
A Maddening Disregard for the Passage of Time (11/17/89 – 5/20/90) (published by The Ecstatic Exchange, 2009)
The Heart Falls in Love with Visions of Perfection (6/15/90 – 6/2/91)
Like When You Wave at a Train and the Train Hoots Back at You (Farid's Book) (6/11 – 7/26/91) (published by The Ecstatic Exchange, 2008)
Orpheus Meets Morpheus (8/1/91 – 3/14/92)
The Puzzle (3/21/92 – 8/17/93)
The Greater Vehicle (10/17/93 – 4/30/94)
A Hundred Little 3-D Pictures (5/14/94 – 9/11/95)
The Angel Broadcast (9/29 – 12/17/95)
Mecca/Medina Time-Warp (12/19/95 – 1/6/96) (published as a Zilzal Press chapbook, 1996)(published in Sparrow on the Prophet's Tomb, 2009)
Miracle Songs for the Millennium (1/20 – 10/16/96)
The Blind Beekeeper (11/15/96 – 5/30/97) (published 2002 by Jusoor/Syracuse University Press)
Chants for the Beauty Feast (6/3 – 10/28/97)(published by The Ecstatic Exchange, 2011)
You Open a Door and it's a Starry Night (10/29/97 – 5/23/98) (published by The Ecstatic Exchange, 2009)
Salt Prayers (5/29 – 10/24/98) (published by The Ecstatic Exchange, 2005)
Some (10/25/98 – 4/25/99)
Flight to Egypt (5/1 – 5/16/99)
I Imagine a Lion (5/21 – 11/15/99) (published by The Ecstatic Exchange, 2006)
Millennial Prognostications (11/25/99 – 2/2/2000) (published by the Ecstatic Exchange, 2009)
Shaking the Quicksilver Pool (2/4 – 10/8/2000) (published by The Ecstatic Exchange, 2009)
Blood Songs (10/9/2000 – 4/3/2001)
The Music Space (4/10 – 9/16/2001) (published by The Ecstatic Exchange, 2007)
Where Death Goes (9/20/2001 – 5/1/2002) (published by The Ecstatic Exchange, 2009)
The Flame of Transformation Turns to Light (99 Ghazals Written in English) (5/14 – 8/21/2002) (published by The Ecstatic Exchange, 2007)

Through Rose-Colored Glasses (7/22/2002 – 1/15/2003) (published by The Ecstatic Exchange, 2007)
Psalms for the Broken-Hearted (1/22 – 5/25/2003) (published by The Ecstatic Exchange, 2006)
Hoopoe's Argument (5/27 – 9/18/03)
Love is a Letter Burning in a High Wind (9/21 – 11/6/2003) (published by The Ecstatic Exchange, 2006)
Laughing Buddha/Weeping Sufi (11/7/2003 – 1/10/2004) (published by The Ecstatic Exchange, 2005)
Mars and Beyond (1/20 – 3/29/2004) (published by The Ecstatic Exchange, 2005)
Underwater Galaxies (4/5 – 7/21/2004) (published by The Ecstatic Exchange, 2007)
Cooked Oranges (7/23/2004 – 1/24/2005 (published by The Ecstatic Exchange, 2007)
Holiday from the Perfect Crime (1/25 – 6/11/2005)(published by The Ecstatic Exchange, 2011)
Stories Too Fiery to Sing Too Watery to Whisper (6/13 – 10/24/2005)
Coattails of the Saint (10/26/2005 – 5/10/2006) (published by The Ecstatic Exchange, 2006)
In the Realm of Neither (5/14/2006 – 11/12/06) (published by The Ecstatic Exchange, 2008)
Invention of the Wheel (11/13/06 – 6/10/07)(published by The Ecstatic Exchange, 2010)
The Sound of Geese Over the House (6/15 – 11/4/07)
The Fire Eater's Lunchbreak (11/11/07 – 5/19/2008) (published by The Ecstatic Exchange, 2008)
Sparks Off the Main Strike (5/24/2008 – 1/10/2009)(published by The Ecstatic Exchange, 2010)
Stretched Out on Amethysts (1/13 – 9/17/2009)(published by The Ecstatic Exchange, 2010)
The Throne Perpendicular to All that is Horizontal (9/18/09 – 1/25/10)
In Constant Incandescence (2/10 – 8/13/10) (published by The Ecstatic Exchange, 2011)
The Caged Bear Spies the Angel (8/30/10 – 3/6/11)(published by The Ecstatic Exchange, 2010)
This Light Slants Upward (3/7/11 –)

www.ingramcontent.com/pod-product-compliance
Lightning Source LLC
Chambersburg PA
CBHW032044150426
43194CB00006B/416